MW00958626

THE PERIODIC TABLE
– *of* –
GOALTENDING ELEMENTS

written by **Justin Goldman**
designed by **Kathy Polo**
edited by **Ken Devine**

Copyright © 2017 by Justin Goldman

All rights reserved. This book or any portion thereof may not be reproduced or used in any manner whatsoever without the expressed written permission of the publisher, except for the use of brief quotations in a book review, website article, or similar journal. This book was written by Justin Goldman and designed by Kathy Polo. All content included in this manuscript is original literature produced by the authors. Elements co-authored by select contributors are notarized within.

First Printing: June, 2017

Quotes are taken from various sources, including books like The Power Within, Embracing The Grind, Between Two Worlds, and The Game.

ISBN-13: 9781546518266
ISBN-10: 1546518266

"To every kid who falls in love with the gear and wears the pads for the first time. May you embrace the goaltending position with passion and integrity, and may it bring you a lifetime of happiness in return."

– Justin Goldman, author

———

"For every boy and girl who wishes to study the art of the goaltending position. May your access to an education never be barred; may your passion for the game never be buried."

– Kathy Polo, designer

A Thank You Note

"The secret of life is to plant without the knowledge that you will harvest.
You plant with the knowledge that others will harvest." — Dr. Don Mattera

Everything we did for this project, we did for the sake of educating and inspiring others.

Born out of this mutual desire, we joined forces in order to create something that would plant seeds of passion for goaltending (and hockey) in people of all ages and walks of life.

We also wanted to focus on holistic development. For there is no greater accomplishment than creating something that motivates another human being to reach for new heights. Progress requires competition to thrive, so we hope the **Periodic Table of Goaltending Elements** will inspire you to study (or teach) the position in new and creative ways.

But the opportunity to create this book and its accompanying learning tools wouldn't exist without a successful Kickstarter campaign. Backed by the financial support of more than 80 generous goalie geeks, we raised over $8,000 and blew right past our fundraising goals, which speaks volumes about the type of passionate and loyal people you will find in the goaltending community.

We're also extremely grateful for the many friends, mentors and pro goalie coaches that provided valuable feedback and contributions to the project. What originally started as a rudimentary infographic back in 2011 continues to grow thanks to these individuals and readers like you.

While it is impossible to reflect the true beauty of goaltending in a single piece of literature, we believe this book will stoke the flames of your puck-stopping passion. Even though the position is complex and the game is changing on a daily basis, a simple rule forever remains; no matter who you are or where you come from, goaltending is for anyone and everyone.

For goaltending, just like science, is truly Universal. There's an endless amount of beauty in both, and there's no limit to what you can achieve when you simply choose to believe.

– Justin & Kathy

The Backers

We would like to extend a special thanks to all of the generous Backers that supported our Kickstarter campaign. Without their generous financial support, this book would not exist!

Paul Alarcon
Scott Appleton
David Bean
Caty Beel
Gustav Bergh
Carson Bird
Matthew Bourgeois
Tom Breunig
Chad Brinson
Stephen Cerutti
Pat Clarke
Marc Crecelius
Matt Davis
Steve Derkach
Jeremy Dickens
Travis Disher
Jarred Drickler-Bourgart
Eric Edmondson
Lantis Escudo
Ian Fleming
Tom Fogu
Matt Forman
"G"
Tiia Goldman

Daniel Hämmerle
Christopher Howard
Paul Huebner
Jaana Inkeroinen
Jacob Kaltenbronn
Greg Kemble
Ian Komorowski
Mitch Korn
David Kovářík
Kelsey Kumpula
Steven Lindland
Alison Lukan
David Marc
Kevin McClure
Cal McConnell
James A. McElligott
Bob McFarlane
Doug McLean
Chase Myers
Jeff Meyers
Andreas Nilsson
Mark O'Reilly
Ray Petkau
Nick Petraglia

Christopher Petz
Chris Poole
Britt Price
James Reodica
El Ricardo
Lisa Roberts
Zachary "Stonewall" Rogers
SchoylarQ
Haley Schultz
Peter Sharpe
Shayne
Scott Smith
Rebecca Stuckey
Jake Sullivan
Jenna Traut
Kevin Travers
Carlos Valdez
Ben Walmsley
Josh Watkins
Cris White
"xmxm"
Veskari

The Contributors

We would also like to thank our project's Contributors. Without their great support and feedback, including their help with the table's overall structure, the organization of the categories, and more specifically, defining the elements listed below, this book would still be in draft mode.

David Alexander: Box Control
Caty Beel: Positioning
Matthew Bourgeois: Blocking
Brian Daccord: Longbody
Steve Derkach: Situational Awareness
Chris Dyson: Character
Jim Graham: Stick
Daniel Pyke: Rotations

Justin Grant: Confidence
Adam Gronlund: Squareness
Mitch Harris: Tracking
Paul Helenski: Battling, Focus
Ray Jean: Rebounds
Joe Messina: Have A Purpose
Len Perno: Anticipation
Dave Stathos: Egoless

Total Funds Raised: $8,140

Book Funding Goal: **$3,000**
Wall Posters Goal: **$5,000**
Flash Cards Goal: **$7,500**

Table of Contents

Table of Contents

Introduction

The Art of Goaltending is driven by three main pillars of human intelligence and interaction: the evolving playing styles, the various training methods, and how we share ideas with one another. The Goaltender's canvas? A clean piece of ice, painted with a colorful palette of graceful movements and core concepts in science, physics, geometry, sports psychology, and more.

Across the globe, the number of children discovering a passion and love for goaltending is on the rise. Grassroots programs are sprouting up in more regions and reaching more demographics than ever before (welcome to the NHL, Las Vegas). Goalie coaching is also growing at a rapid pace, bringing with it a stronger focus and financial commitment to national development programs. As a result, the goaltending culture has reached a point where it is more prominent, in-depth, and "position specific" than ever before.

The biggest downfall? Goaltending is an expensive endeavor, so playing at a competitive level is not always easy. The gear, the training, the traveling, and the annual team fees quickly reach a point where it eliminates a large percentage of the general population from the talent pool. It is also a complex position, one full of many different terms, teaching methods, and styles. In fact, just getting coaches to agree on a similar and consistent language has been an ongoing battle.

Simply put, goaltending is not without its fair share of obstacles.

Therefore, it is our duty as educators, coaches, and parents to provide today's enthusiastic young hockey fans with affordable and accessible educational tools. These tools should not only improve their on-ice skills, but also important life skills like self-awareness, time management, creativity, and intelligence.

With this duty in mind, allow us to introduce you to the **Periodic Table of Goaltending Elements**.

The Table Structure

Whether you're a hockey player, a student, or a parent, the odds are high that you've seen the scientific Periodic Table of Elements once or twice before. If so, then you can probably tell what this project is all about. If you haven't seen it before, then prepare for a fun learning experience that will help you grasp and master the fundamentals of the greatest position in sports!

No matter what you're made of, the scientific Elements help define the world you live in. They bring meaning to your five senses, they create your reality, and they mix together in different ways to create every single thing (and person) on the earth.

Similarly, this periodic table educates readers on the many "elements" of goaltending. What are the things or skills that make goalies unique from other athletes? What ingredients, both visible and invisible, do you need to be a good goalie? How are these skills organized? What happens when they mix together? How can they be arranged in a way that makes you a better goalie? Before we can help you answer those questions, we want to make sure you understand how our periodic table works! Let's start by taking you through the table's structure.

The Four Categories

Made in the image and likeness of the traditional scientific version, this periodic table includes 131 of the most common performance-related terms found in the goaltending dictionary. That means the primary focus of this book is on a goalie's abilities, skills, behaviors, and talents.

Elements are organized into four different categories: **Physical**, **Mental**, **Technical**, and **Tactical**. The **Physical Skills** are related to the body, like **Strength [St]** and **Flexibility [Fx]**. **The Mental Skills** are related to the mind, like **Confidence [C]** and being **Relaxed [Rx]**. The **Technical Skills** are related to the fundamentals, like **Recoveries [Rc]** and the **Butterfly [Bf]**. Finally, **Tactical Skills** are related to advanced strategies and skills, like **Box Control [Bx]**.

It's important to understand that many goaltending elements will have multiple definitions and meanings, an effect we call **Crossover.** As a result, our periodic table is a **Dynamic** one (the opposite of **Static**) and open to the reader's interpretation. That means you can move elements around and rearrange them however you'd like without changing its overall purpose and integrity.

TACTICAL

PHYSICAL

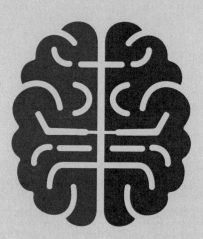

MENTAL

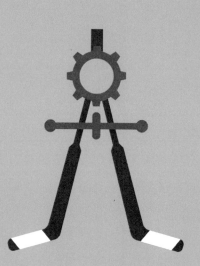

TECHNICAL

The Groups

Next, let's discuss the organization of the 131 elements. The nine (9) horizontal rows are called **Periods**, whereas the eighteen (18) vertical columns are referred to as **Groups**. In order to try and simplify the learning process, the table's orientation and structure is focused on the 18 groups.

For example, the goalie's **Stance [P]** is considered a fundamental or "keystone" element in the Physical category. Every save movement originates from the goalie's Stance, and a proper stance will result in good body **Alignment [A]** and posture. That in turn results in better **Coverage [Cv]** for whatever type of stance you use or shot you may face.

If we look at column 16, **Vision [V]** is the fundamental physical skill needed to continually see and follow the puck, or what is commonly known as **Tracking [T]**. From there, a goalie must rely on their vision skills by developing a skill known as **Reading Plays [Re]**. From there, honing your **Peripheral Vision [Pv]** allows you to watch players become passing targets or see scoring threats.

Just like the table as a whole is dynamic in form, so too are the 18 Groups. So remember, the logical flow of each column is merely an example; there are no right or wrong answers. Treat this like a guide to help you discover more about yourself and your own interpretations of goaltending!

How to Study the Table

Through the use of our full-color learning book, coaches, kids, and parents alike can study the goaltending position by breaking it down into its individual components and basic fundamentals.

The book also includes a small sample of workbook-style reflection exercises. From coloring pages to building your own periodic table, these were added to promote further learning in a variety of settings. It's also an example of what you will find on The Goalie Guild as time goes on; new exercises will be added as time goes on for you to download free of charge!

But our project does not stop there. Beyond the book, we've also created a full-color wall poster, a set of printable flash-cards, and even an online studying app to promote even more learning!

The Poster: Our full-color posters of the periodic table can be purchased on The Goalie Guild's website and shipped to you in a variety of sizes and formats. Hang it on a wall in your bedroom, somewhere in your local hockey rink, or inside your goalie training center. It will catch people's attention and become a great conversation-starter! Keep a few copies of this book and the flash cards nearby, and watch how young kids and hockey parents come to appreciate its uses!

The Flash Cards: A set of our flash cards can also be purchased on The Goalie Guild website. These are a great way to study the elements while also promoting hockey to fans everywhere! Use them to pass the time on those lengthy tournament road trips, give a set as a birthday gift to the goalie in your family, or challenge your friends to see who can memorize the most elements!

If you'd like to purchase posters or flash cards, please visit www.TheGoalieGuild.com and order them at any time. If you are interested in buying more than 10 sets of any particular item, a bulk discount price is also available.

Promoting Creativity

One of the goals we have for this project is to stimulate and develop **Creativity** in readers. Creativity is essential to goaltending because it allows you to discover new and different ways to stop the puck, make unorthodox saves, or come up with unique drills in practice. This ability to think "outside the box" and come up with new solutions for the many situations you will face as a goalie can also benefit you in school, at the office, and even on the playground!

For these reasons, the book and additional learning tools are made to be multi-functional and flexible; you can use them in a variety of ways. The more ways you can study the position using our learning tools, the more chances you'll have to strengthen your problem-solving skills, confidence, character, and even your performance levels in games and practices!

To give you an example of how you can strengthen your creativity skills, consider the following questions:

Which elements would you move, relocate, or remove from our version of the periodic table? Which elements do you think belong in a different category? What would your version of the table look like? Are we missing any key elements or terms that you use on a regular basis? How can you use this book, the poster, or the flash cards with your teammates, parents, or coaches?

When you're done studying the elements, take some time to complete the workbook exercises, and then share your work on our social media accounts (**@TheGoalieGuild** on Twitter, Facebook, and Instagram) so that we can showcase your work to all of our followers.

Now that you know the purpose, structure, and methods for using the Periodic Table of Goaltending Elements, it's time to start studying!

Remember, there are no wrong answers, so **be creative** and more importantly, have **fun with it!** The options are endless and the only limitations are the ones you place on yourself!

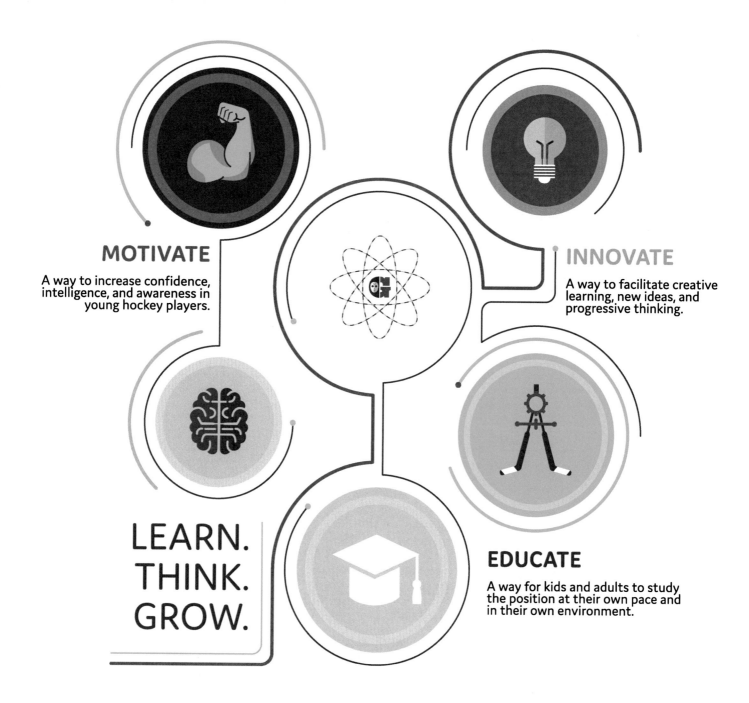

MOTIVATE

A way to increase confidence, intelligence, and awareness in young hockey players.

INNOVATE

A way to facilitate creative learning, new ideas, and progressive thinking.

LEARN.
THINK.
GROW.

EDUCATE

A way for kids and adults to study the position at their own pace and in their own environment.

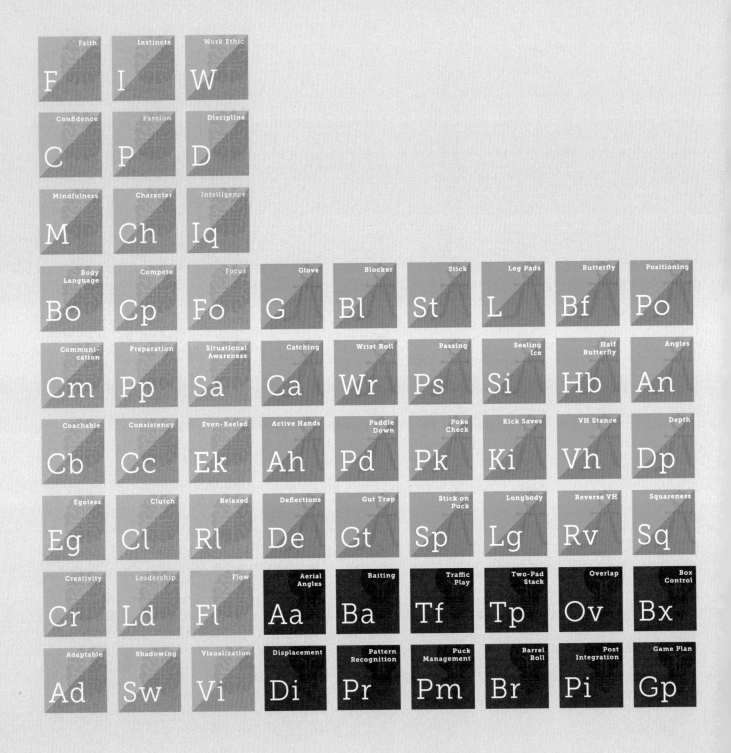

							Athleticism A	**Stance** S
Vision V	**Footwork** Ft	**Quickness** Q	**Balance** B	**Reflexes** Rx	**Alignment** Al			
Tracking T	**Skating** Sk	**Size** Sz	**Coordination** Co	**Flexibility** Fx	**Coverage** Cv			

Save Selections Sv	**Rebounds** R	**Recoveries** Rc	**Reading Plays** Re	**Edges** E	**Strength** Sg	**Rhythm** Rh	**Agility** Ag	**Sealing Holes** Sh
Blocking Bk	**Butterfly Slide** Bs	**Rotations** Ro	**Peripheral Vision** Pv	**Lateral Adjustment** Lt	**Durability** Du	**Body Control** Bc	**Dexterity** Dx	**Compact** Ct
Challenge Cg	**Backside Push** Bp	**Weight Transfer** Wt	**Save Selections** Sv	**Hop-Step** Hs	**Battling** Bt	**Shifting** Sf	**Explosive** Ex	**Efficiency** Ef
Transitions Ts	**Shoulder Shrugs** Ss	**Knee Walks** Kn	**Reading Releases** Rr	**Heel Lift** Hl	**Desperation** Ds	**Dynamic** Dy	**Second Efforts** Se	**Economical** Ec
Nudges Ng	**Bumps** Bu	**Pop-Up Recovery** Pu	**Head Trajectory** Ht	**Micro Adjustments** Ma	**Scrambling** Sb	**Anticipation** Ai	**Contorting** Cn	**Spatial Recognition** Sr
Gap Control Gc	**Hinging** Hi	**Adaptive Skating** As	**Quiet Eye** Qe	**Angle Management** Am	**Energy Management** Em	**Patience** Pt	**Breathing** Bg	**Kinesthetic Sense** Ks

PHYSICAL

"

"The toughest part about the job is the daily grind, but at the same time, you enjoy it. You get your schedule and your routine. Practice, play, practice, play. I enjoy that part of the game."

– JONATHAN QUICK

PHYSICAL

ATHLETICISM

The ability to use the physical tools needed to play the position. These tools–which are a collection of different skills like balance, body control, speed, skating, and power–work together in different ways to perform the wide spectrum of goaltending movements. Unlike athletes in other sports who need to reach extremes, goaltenders focus on their ability to get into the proper position so that extreme or excessive movements aren't needed. One way to develop a more dynamic and well-rounded athletic base is by playing other sports and participating in other activities!

STANCE

The point of origin for your positioning and the way in which your body parts are placed when at a standstill. There are many types of stances in the goaltending dictionary, including the basic stance, ready stance, and relaxed stance. In some parts of the world, namely Sweden, a stance is also considered any set position of the body, including the Reverse VH and the paddle-down. Knowing how to use all of the stances in your toolbox—and when to use them—is not only one of the main principles of successful goaltending, but is constantly being refined.

THE PERIODIC TABLE – of – GOALTENDING ELEMENTS

PHYSICAL

"Everybody should have that motivation to be the best at what they do. If I am or if I'm not, it's relevant to what other people think; it's what I believe." – Olaf Kolzig

VISION

The ability to see the game. Vision is one of the most important skills in goaltending because you can't stop what you can't see. A strong visual system is a trait that all goalies need in order to properly read and react to the game. Since you must be able to focus on a constantly moving puck or use your peripheral vision to locate threats, vision training should be a part of your training routine and long-term development. Your eyes are muscles, so you can condition and strengthen them at any age to work better and more effectively!

FOOTWORK

The ability to alter your positioning, net coverage, or stance by moving your feet in a quick and efficient manner. As a core element that influences the way a goalie moves, footwork is simply known as the behavior of the feet and the ability to move them in different ways. Goalies should spend some time every day working on their feet, whether they're on the ice or in the weight room. By improving your foot strength and agility on a daily basis, your footwork will become one of the key skills that drives your success and gives you the edge over other goalies.

PHYSICAL

QUICKNESS

The ability to move or change your position as fast as possible. Quickness is a key element that allows some goalies to travel with more speed than others, thus making them more effective when repositioning their body or reacting to shots. Because there are many speeds (alteration speed, reaction speed, cognitive speed, and processing speed) quickness encompasses all aspects of being an athlete. It's a key aspect of goaltending, but remember that you can't improve your speed until you've first learned the technique!

BALANCE

The ability to create and maintain an even distribution of weight in order to achieve stable positioning and posture. This is achieved when your body combines proper alignment with your center of gravity. Balance requires coordination from numerous sensory systems, including vision and what is known as proprioception. Balance is also used regularly by goalie coaches to teach a key aspect of the mental game. It's extremely important that goalies strive for life balance by playing other sports, having other hobbies, and not focusing all of their energy on hockey!

PHYSICAL

"If you keep doing the right things, keep working the right way, and do what you are supposed to do to prepare, then good things will happen. What goes around comes around. You get what you deserve." – Johan Hedberg

REFLEXES

The involuntary movements that take place when you play the game. Scientifically speaking, a reflex is a triggered response to stimuli, so it is directly related to a goalie's instincts through the work of the central nervous system. Reflexes fall under the category of athleticism because they act as the main product of all basic movements needed for successful goaltending. Your reflexes will naturally improve over time as you gain more experience and fine motor skills, but you can develop them by playing in an open environment. Just go out and play, and your reflexes will improve!

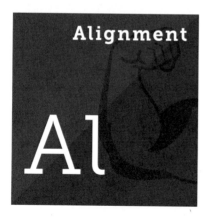

ALIGNMENT

The optimal placement of your body parts. When your body has proper alignment in your stance, your skeletal and muscular system can act and react efficiently. You can also achieve alignment by having good posture, which alleviates strain and tension from your muscles and helps you make better movements. A great way to visualize the importance of alignment is to think of your body as a dangling chain made up of many links. Since everything in your body is connected from top to bottom, even one weak or faulty link can have a negative impact on the strength of other links, and thus the chain as a whole.

PHYSICAL

TRACKING

The ability to keep your eyes on the puck. This fundamental goaltending skill is comprised of three parts. The first is tracking the play, which includes watching the puck as it moves around the ice. The second part is tracking the shot, which begins just before the puck is released off the shooter's stick blade. Goalies must continue to track the puck by watching it all the way into their body. That leads to the third part, which is tracking the rebound as it travels away from your body. At this point, the process repeats and the tracking continues!

SKATING

The ability to move and propel your body around the ice. Skating is one of the main principles of goaltending because you can't stop the puck if you can't move your feet. Basic skating is broken down into three simple movements: the shuffle, the C-cut, and the T-push. Shuffles are small side-to-side pushes made in a straight line. C-cuts are small C-shaped swivels of the foot that allow you to move forward or backward. T-pushes are used to travel longer distances. Mastering all three movements in any direction is critical to your success, so practice them every day!

PHYSICAL

"I always had the mindset when I was playing that I was going to be the hardest worker, that I was going to do more than everyone else out there, and just not give up on my dream." - Jordan Sigalet

SIZE

The dimensions and overall size of a goalie's body. Size may not be an ability unto itself, but how you use your size is an important skill for all goalies. Size not only includes your height and weight, but also the length of different limbs and bones—like your arms, legs, thighs, and feet. Size is a great asset at the highest levels, but smaller goalies can be just as successful as bigger goalies if they have great positioning and athleticism. Always remember that bigger doesn't always mean better; it's not the size of the body that matters, but the strength of the mind!

COORDINATION

The combination of body movements—both conscious and unconscious—needed to create an action or reaction. Coordination occurs whenever a goalie's limbs move in a manner that is well-timed, smooth, and efficient. This includes the gathering and processing of information leading up to the coordinated movement, as well as the natural execution of the body's neuromuscular system. Synergy is another term often that's often used when discussing the more advanced sports science of motor coordination and different biomechanics, such as eye-hand coordination.

PHYSICAL

FLEXIBILITY

The range of motion in all joints in the body. Flexibility is considered a predisposed trait because it's determined by a combination of many natural factors, like age and genetics. You can improve your flexibility with proper stretching, but you can also lose it from living a lazy lifestyle. No matter your age or genetics, you can always increase your range of motion through various functional movement disciplines like yoga and Pilates!

COVERAGE

The manner in which you fill open space in relation to the puck and the 6-by-4-foot goal frame. This includes not only the way in which you wear your equipment, but where you place your hands, feet, and body. Essentially, coverage describes the relationship between time and space, thus tying it to depth, angles, and positioning. Because everyone's body is slightly different, like snowflakes in a winter storm, no two goalies create the same exact coverage. Tall or short, your ability to understand how much space you're covering will play a huge role in your development.

PHYSICAL

"Everybody plans on being a starting goalie in the NHL, but it's not a reality for a lot of us. I think you have to realize that you're fortunate to have made it to this level and realize you're a part of something that is bigger than you." – Curtis McElhinney

Strength

Sg

STRENGTH

The ability to generate force and power with the muscles in your body. Stamina, which is the physical endurance and sustained energy of a goalie's body, is another key component of strength. Broken down even further, strength is the goalie's ability to push, pull, and stabilize their body when moving around the crease. Goalies with good strength can seal their foot to the post and hold the goal line with their pad, make quality passes and clears off the glass, use their core strength to make stable and controlled movements, and much more!

Rhythm

Rh

RHYTHM

The ability to perform a sequence of movements with proper timing. Rhythm is a fundamental aspect of developing quality skills in young athletes and is a key principle found in every sport. By learning the individual pieces that make up a sequence, rhythm can be improved by actually feeling the transition from one movement to the next. There are many ways to improve your rhythm as a goalie, including jumping rope or doing drills that require consistent, fast-paced repetition— like catching pucks in a specific pattern, or butterfly-sliding back and forth like a swinging pendulum.

PHYSICAL

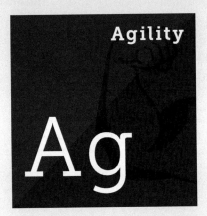

Agility

Ag

AGILITY

The ability to adjust or alter your body and positioning in an effective manner. Combined with other physical skills like balance, coordination, and speed, this element allows you to rapidly isolate and move different body parts. Goalies constantly rely on their agility for many movements, such as changing directions, making lateral adjustments, and transferring their weight during butterfly slides. Agility is linked to athleticism, as both are mutually beneficial to successful goaltending; the more you improve one, the more you improve the other.

Sealing
Holes

Sh

SEALING HOLES

The ability to keep pucks from squeezing through or slipping under you by eliminating tiny holes in your save selection. Sealing off the 6-hole and 7-hole (the space between your arms and body) is vital to successful goaltending, but it takes good body and spatial awareness to truly master. The better you get at feeling and understanding the way your body takes up space, the better you'll be at making the subtle and slight movements needed to eliminate those tiny holes and keep the puck out of the net!

PHYSICAL

"I would always ask myself, 'do you like to practice?' And I always enjoy going to practice, and that's why I never quit." - Tim Thomas

DURABILITY

The ability to endure lengthy periods of action or an excessive workload while still showing focus, poise, and efficiency. Durability also refers to a goalie's ability to manage physical or mental strain by exhibiting a combination of strength and agility without suffering from energy drain or laziness. Durability is not just how strong you are, but what type of pain thresholds you can endure and how far you're willing to push yourself in order to withstand the rigors and stresses of goaltending.

BODY CONTROL

The ability to direct, maneuver, and stabilize any part of your body when playing the position. Body control is a key physical skill for goalies of all ages because it's fundamental for establishing good positioning and making efficient movements. By having a good athletic base to work from, goalies are able to move as one solid unit, with stable arms and hands in front of their body, as well as proper stick placement. Developing stronger core muscles will help your body control, but it will also improve naturally over time as you gain experience.

PHYSICAL

Dexterity

Dx

DEXTERITY

The ability to use your hands, gloves, and stick with precision and grace. Since goalies get a feel for the puck with their hands, dexterity includes anything related to altering and manipulating your palms, wrists, and forearms in order to improve biomechanics when making glove saves or handling the puck. Dexterity incorporates alteration speed, reaction speed, and processing speed, therefore including the Mental and Tactical categories in addition to the Physical. You can improve your hand dexterity by juggling and doing many other eye-hand exercises.

Compact

Ct

COMPACT

The ability to eliminate holes under your arms or between your legs by condensing your body into a tighter and more solid unit. The term "compact" or "tight" is often used by goalie coaches to explain when a goalie collapses their arms, legs, and/or knees toward their core in order to make a narrow or gathered save. You can form a compact stance by bringing or setting all parts of your body in a more narrowed position, or by bringing everything closer together—as opposed to having a wider and more spread-out stance.

PHYSICAL

"All I worry about is making that first save, and when you're doing that it really simplifies things." – Carey Price

Battling

Bt

BATTLING

The ability to work extra hard in order to see the puck and make a save. Goalies who battle have a high compete level, fighting to stop every shot and never giving up on a play—no matter the odds. While battling, opponents will often push or brush into you, making it very hard to stay in position or keep a good stance. Your teammates will often move in front of you as well, blocking your sight. When these disruptions happen, you must use all of your skills to make sure you can still see the puck and move properly. A goalie who can make saves when it isn't easy is called a "battler" because they're always willing to pay the price in order to stop the puck!

Shifting

Sf

SHIFTING

The ability to shift or lean your body in the direction of a shot's trajectory in order to improve your net coverage. A common shift happens in the Reverse VH, when you lean your shoulder into the post to take away more space in the upper corner of the goal frame. Shifting can also refer to "center-shifting," which is when a goalie drops down into a tight butterfly but makes a slight lateral adjustment, thus shifting into the shot lane without opening up holes or overreaching. When you shift, make sure you always do it in a calm, quiet, and controlled manner.

PHYSICAL

EXPLOSIVE

The ability to move with an extremely powerful first step, stride, reaction, or movement. This takes strength, relaxed muscles, and an ability to use your inside edges to get from one point to the next as quickly as possible. Explosiveness is a sign of good blade engagement, body control, and reactions. Goalie coaches are always looking for explosive movements because they show that you're moving with a purpose and with a chance to beat the pass or get set and square without falling behind the play.

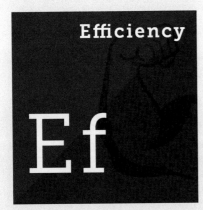

EFFICIENCY

The ability to execute minor movements and reactions fluidly and in the quickest, most effective manner possible. Scientifically, efficiency is defined as "the economy of force exertion and energy expenditure." This is achieved when you have a perfect balance of sufficient muscle stimulation and restraint in order to move as effortlessly as possible. Although the Efficiency element is similar to the Economical one in the broader sense, efficiency is different because it's mainly related to how a goalie is evaluated under the individual components and biomechanics of goaltender movements and reactions.

PHYSICAL

"You put on years when you put on a goaltender's equipment. A twenty-year-old kid is suddenly middle-aged when he's got that stuff on."
– Ted Green

Desperation

Ds

DESPERATION

The ability to abandon your comfort zone in order to make a timely save in an urgent or uncontrolled manner. Desperation is often considered a state of mind rather than a technical term, but it still includes the execution of physical and technical elements at a frenzied or hurried pace in order to make a save. Desperation saves can include diving, sliding, extending, reaching back, or any other extreme movement born out of sheer will or desire. They can be taught in a structured manner and practiced in a controlled setting.

Dynamic

Dy

DYNAMIC

The ability to exhibit a wide range of movements, reactions, and athletic tools. Dynamic goaltenders are capable of moving their body in unique ways in order to make saves in whatever situation is presented to them. Dynamic goalies also benefit from their unpredictability—the more ways they can stop the puck, the harder it is for a shooter to read their style and for an opposing team to scout their tendencies. You can improve your dynamic movements by dedicating time to increasing your flexibility, athleticism, and range of motion.

PHYSICAL

SECOND EFFORTS

The ability to make a save attempt after you've already committed to making the initial save. Second efforts take place when there's no chance for a basic or routine recovery, or when you lack the ability to get set and square up to a rebound shot. Second efforts are a sign of competitiveness, battling, and raw athleticism. Even if you're totally down and out on a play, never give up on the puck and always try to get a piece of it, even if you're caught swimming in the crease!

ECONOMICAL

The ability to achieve perfect net coverage and full squareness to the puck with conservative positioning and shorter movements. By having perfect body control and eliminating any delay or over-sliding, economical goalies move in whatever method results in straight lines and optimal pushes. The economy of movement is often seen when watching Carey Price, as he's the textbook example of this ability and mindset. It's also important to remember that, depending on the puck's location, even the slightest movement—like a lean or shift—can be excessive.

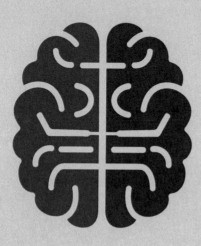

MENTAL

"

"Because the demands on the goalie are mostly mental, it means that for a goalie the biggest enemy is himself. Not a puck, not a opponent, not a quirk of size or style. The stress and anxiety he feels when he plays, the fear of failing, the fear of being embarrassed, the fear of being physically hurt, all symptoms of his position, in constant ebb and flow, but never disappearing. The successful goalie understands these neuroses, accept them, and put them under control. The unsuccessful goalie is distracted by them, his mind in knots. His body quickly follows."

– KEN DRYDEN

MENTAL

"There is no position in sport as noble as goaltending."
– Vladislav Tretiak

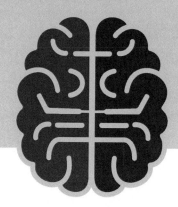

FAITH

The ability to believe in yourself and to trust the process in attaining your goals. No matter who you are or where you're from, your faith is what inspires and motivates you to do anything or be anyone you want. Faith is the first element in our periodic table because your faith and personal beliefs lay the foundation for a happy and meaningful life. Just like a rocket ship that needs fuel to reach deep space, faith is the fuel that allows any goalie to reach for the stars and make their dreams a reality. If you have confidence in yourself and an unwavering faith in the process, absolutely anything is possible!

INSTINCTS

The ability to make reads and reactions without needing to think about them. On a scientific level, instincts are all of your natural-born physical and mental athletic behaviors. These behaviors are actions or thoughts that transpire on an unconscious level, so instincts are not skills that can be easily acquired. Your instincts are developed over months and even years of repetitive training. "Trust yourself" and "Just go out there and play" are sayings that are often used to help goalies rely on their instincts.

MENTAL

WORK ETHIC

The ability to work hard in all areas of the game. Your work ethic is a set of character traits that reflect your ability to do whatever it takes to accomplish a goal. It's a major key to your success because it proves that you have a purpose and a passion for life. Work ethic is often defined by how much grit and determination you put into different areas of your life, especially when nobody is watching. It plays a huge role in defining your identity, and since your attitude determines your altitude, goalies must always come to the rink ready to give it their all—no matter the cost!

CONFIDENCE

The quality of believing in yourself and your ability to stop the puck. With full faith in your skills and your game plan, confidence can grow just like the muscles in your body. It's strengthened by dedicating time to your craft on the ice and working hard off the ice. If you choose to build confidence in these ways and can say "I'm good at this!" to yourself, then your confidence will rise. The feeling you get from a boost in confidence is one of comfort; it's a sureness in your abilities. A confident goalie can outplay a more skilled goalie anytime or anywhere, so always believe in yourself and trust the process, no matter how hard things get!

MENTAL

"That's what body language can do; it can transcend and transform a whole team. If you want to grow and move on and be at your ultimate best, you have to take care of your body language." – Marty Turco

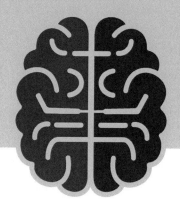

PASSION

Having an unyielding love for hockey and goaltending. Passion is the lifeblood of the body, mind, and spirit; it is the natural and unquenchable desire to stop pucks, improve your skill, and win games. Without a true passion for the game, achieving great things is not possible. Passion is the fuel that drives your engine, the power within you, and the essence of your competitive nature. It is one of the most indestructible forces that exists inside of you, and it can sustain you for an entire lifetime. Passion promotes success and is a pillar of life!

DISCIPLINE

The ability to exhibit willpower over your mind and control over your body. This includes the ability to manipulate and direct decisions, reactions, work ethic, and behaviors in a manner that allows you to fully control your actions and reactions. Discipline is also a goalie's ability to manage their attitude and personality in a moral and positive manner. On a physical plane, when an action takes place somewhere in your body, discipline is your body's ability to control and direct the response. It takes years of great training discipline to reach the NHL.

MENTAL

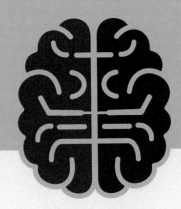

MINDFULNESS

The ability to be aware of your surroundings, actions, and responsibilities as a goalie. This includes a wide range of mental and emotional skills, including the ability to avoid distractions, to control your anger or fear, and to understand another person's point of view. Mindfulness also includes the full range of attitudes and beliefs that develop your holistic skills, like preparation, motivation, and being a good teammate. Mindfulness may not have a big influence on your game at a younger age, but start creating this good habit now because it will definitely play a key role when you're older!

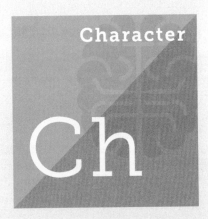

CHARACTER

The collection of behavioral traits that reflect your ethics and beliefs. Character is often defined as "what you do when nobody is watching" and is your desire to genuinely do or say the right thing. Goalies are natural leaders who should always strive to set a positive example for others and have the morals of someone who is respected by all. Good character means accepting and embracing your role as the last line of defense, never pointing the blame at anyone or anything, striving to be a dutiful servant for your team, and being quietly confident yet humble in all situations.

THE PERIODIC TABLE – *of* – GOALTENDING ELEMENTS

MENTAL

"I want you to know that if you fall in love with the position - if you dream about it...if the position is in your blood and there's no real explanation for it - you have what it takes to make it in hockey." – Garret Sparks

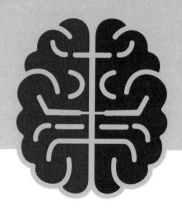

INTELLIGENCE

The ability to learn and understand the finer aspects of goaltending. Intelligence is measured in a number of ways and is not solely judged by book smarts, street smarts, or talent. It can include creativity, problem-solving, recognition, and many other mental and cognitive aspects of success in sports. Goalie IQ is often defined by a goalie's ability to master different technical elements of the position through natural and learned talent. Remember, intelligence is not just how smart you are, but how you use the tools you have to accomplish certain tasks!

BODY LANGUAGE

Any type of nonverbal communication that displays and reveals key information about a goalie. Everything from gestures, facial expressions, posture, and reactions after giving up a goal are visual reflections of your attitude and identity. Who you are as an individual is often defined by what people see you doing in games, practices, and in life away from the rink. As a result, goalies with good body language are able to develop successful habits that can pay huge dividends throughout their careers. Instill good body language habits now, and reap the rewards later!

MENTAL

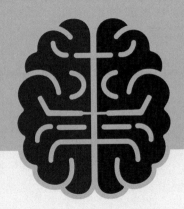

COMPETE

The ability to out-work and out-perform your opponent through sheer will, desire, and effort. A goalie that excels at competing has a high and visible level of determination, work ethic, and focus. "Compete on every shot" is one of the goaltender's main commandments, because it can inspire your teammates and help shift the momentum of a hockey game in your favor. No matter how much talent you may have, adding a little competitive fire to your practice habits will take your game and skills to new heights!

FOCUS

The ability to selectively concentrate on one aspect of your game or surroundings, while blocking out all others. Goalies must be able to channel their attention onto specific tasks at different times, or multi-task by accomplishing different skills at the same time. A goalie with great focus has strong mental acuity skills and a strong ability to process all aspects of the game, both with body and mind. You can improve your focus by being more aware of hockey's many patterns and trends, communicating with your coaches and teammates, and studying all areas of the

MENTAL

"Enjoy the moment, but work every day like it's your last day."
– Fred Brathwaite

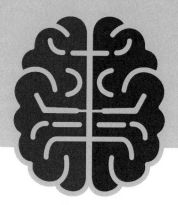

COMMUNICATION

The ability to express and share information with your teammates in an effective manner, both on and off the ice. Communication is vital when managing plays with your defensemen, as they often rely on your verbal cues and hand gestures in order to better defend the zone. From passing the puck to making your teammates aware of a sneaky backdoor threat to notifying the bench that a penalty has just ended, effective communication is crucial to success. Communication is also an essential life skill that extends into your everyday relationships with teammates, coaches, family, and friends, so you can do yourself and others a big favor by practicing good communication every day!

PREPARATION

The ability to achieve mental and physical readiness for a game. A goalie prepares to compete through a routine, which is a set of activities and habits that provides physical comfort and emotional confidence. Every goalie has their own unique routine, but it can take years to truly understand and execute what works best for you. Stretching, warming up your eyes with tennis ball exercises, and listening to music are common ways that goalies prepare. Another popular way to prepare for a big game is by visualizing yourself making good movements and awesome saves!

MENTAL

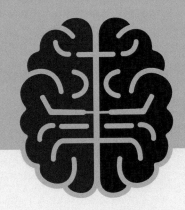

Situational Awareness

Sa

SITUATIONAL AWARENESS

The ability to analyze potential scoring threats while also focusing on the puck and the current play or situation. A goalie's positioning is dynamic and always changing, especially on the smallest of scales and with the slightest movements. In order to read the play properly and make effective saves, you must be aware of all potential outcomes that could arise in any situation, thus giving you more information to help make the appropriate reaction or movement as the play unfolds.

Coachable

Cb

COACHABLE

The ability to be a good student, regardless of the teacher. Whether it's paying attention to instructions or being receptive to learning new techniques, coachable goalies have an open mind, act with a positive attitude, and strive to be the best they can be on and off the ice. They exhibit an energetic and contagious desire to learn and are willing to accept constructive criticism at all times. They're willing to work when fixes need to be made, they listen well to their superiors, they ask questions when they don't understand something, and they're even able to admit when they're wrong.

MENTAL

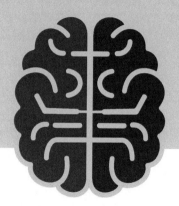

CONSISTENCY

The ability to perform at a high level on a continual basis, regardless of internal or external influences. These factors include both life situations and anything that may transpire in the game of hockey. Although consistency is placed in the Mental category, it exists in the Technical field as well. Consistent movements are key to consistent performances, and it's through discipline, purposeful practice, and repetition that your muscle memory improves. Starting NHL goalies rarely have two bad games in a row, which is a great example of their mental consistency!

EVEN-KEELED

The ability to maintain a steady disposition, regardless of what happens around you. Whether you're feeling on top of the world after a 50-save shutout or suffering from the lows of a long losing streak, being even-keeled means that you continue to stay level-headed and focused on playing your game. Even-keeled goalies never lose control of their emotions, even when a negative response would be justified. When things don't go your way, stay even-keeled and remember that the only thing that truly matters is the next shot!

MENTAL

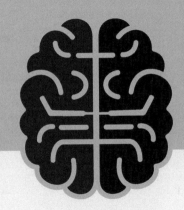

Egoless

Eg

EGOLESS

The ability to embrace an unselfish attitude in all aspects of hockey and life. Egoless goalies are modest and grateful, accepting responsibility and criticism without resistance. They have an ability to lead quietly, and they never put their needs in front of anyone else's. The top priority of an egoless goalie is the team's success, and they understand that they're just a part of the winning equation. They don't seek recognition or attention, but rather use their talents to benefit others. Check your ego at the door before you step into the rink and you'll make everyone around you better!

Clutch

Cl

CLUTCH

The ability to make big saves and come up with game-saving performances in pressure-filled situations. A clutch goalie is focused, poised, and in full control of their body and mind when a team is in desperation mode. Clutch goalies seem to have a knack for finding different ways to make key saves, especially when it's least expected. Clutch goalies are the ones who constantly make big saves in high-percentage scoring situations, like in the final minute of a tight game, when their team is down by a goal, on wide-open 2-on-0 breakaways, or one-on-one in a shootout.

MENTAL

"There are as many styles as there are goalies."
– Thomas Magnusson

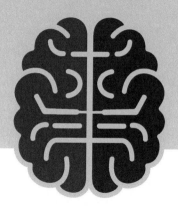

RELAXED

The ability to stay calm under pressure. Relaxed goalies don't feel any tension in their muscles and react fluidly, without any physical or mental hindrances, delays, and hesitations. They're able to quiet their mind and play with a clear conscience. They don't get rattled when giving up a goal or a juicy rebound and they're never worried about external circumstances, things beyond their control, or what others are doing. Proper breathing techniques can help your mind and body relax when the pressure is rising, so always remember to keep calm and carry on!

CREATIVITY

The ability to combine talent, intelligence, and imagination in order to make saves or improve your skills. Creativity is your resourcefulness (also known as cognitive flexibility) and your ability to apply different techniques and tactics in new ways. It's also an ability to think outside the box or play in an unorthodox fashion in order to solve problems. Creativity is a vital part of many goaltending skills, just like your ability to perceive, memorize, imagine, and apply. Creativity also takes ingenuity; goalies love to modify and custom fit their gear in order to move better and stop more pucks!

MENTAL

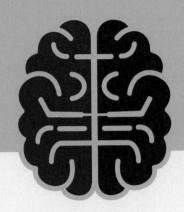

Leadership

Ld

LEADERSHIP

The collection of traits that helps you lead a team and others. Leadership is a combination of attitude, confidence, responsibility, unselfishness, and the power to instill confidence in others. Leadership requires a heavy dose of humility and is a result of having the respect of your teammates, mainly due to your own respect for the game. Leaders never cheat the game or cut corners with their work ethic. They show up with a professional demeanor and put others on their shoulders in order to lift up the entire team.

Flow

Fl

FLOW

The ability to achieve balance between your body, mind, and emotions. Flow is often referred to as a state of mind that you can achieve when your movements, reactions, and thoughts are in perfect harmony with each other. Goalies who achieve a state of flow are often described as playing in the moment and with a relaxed intensity or heightened sense of awareness. Playing with flow is also similar to being "in the zone" or any situation where you feel like everything is clicking, the bounces are in your favor, and every decision or outcome is the desired one.

MENTAL

"Sometimes you can press a little bit and you're trying to do too much and you're trying too hard. You want to win so bad and you want to help the team so badly that you end up trying too much instead of letting the play come to you." – Ed Belfour

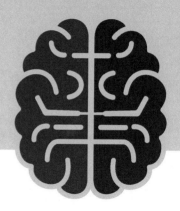

ADAPTABLE

The ability to change or modify your state of mind or style of play in accordance with the current situation. From smaller in-game adjustments to bigger ones made over a longer period of time, goalies must be able to thrive in different surroundings. In order to improve in constantly changing environments, you must always be open to change and be receptive to the unique needs of your body. By developing a deep toolbox, you can adapt to the game and find ways to alter your style in order to match up better against your opponents.

SHADOWING

The ability to mimic the movements and styles of other goalies. Whether you're watching your favorite NHL netminder on TV or spending time on the ice with a mentor, shadowing is a natural ability that allows you to observe and replicate the traits of other goalies. This is done on both a conscious and subconscious level, as you pick up different traits, techniques, and habits throughout your life just by watching others. How you incorporate these traits into your game will naturally influence your development and unique style of play.

MENTAL

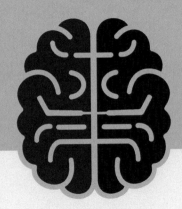

VISUALIZATION

The ability to create a mental image of what you want to feel and accomplish in real life. This popular preparation tactic is often known as guided imagery because you imagine a desired outcome in order to gain a competitive edge. Seeing yourself make saves or win games is a mental rehearsal that serves as a great way to gain experience and boost confidence in your abilities. Most professional goaltenders have incorporated some type of visualization into their routine, and it's a must-have for developing goalies who want to raise their level of play and their ability to perform under pressure.

TECHNICAL

"

"You can't learn and get to where you want to be until you go through the process. It would be so easy to just read it in a book and then know everything [about goaltending] when you're 21 or 22. But it doesn't work that way. You have to listen to your experiences and use them to your advantage."

– TOMAS VOKOUN

THE PERIODIC TABLE – *of* – GOALTENDING ELEMENTS

TECHNICAL

"It doesn't matter if you had a shutout the night before, you should still try to get better the next day. Having the fire to get better every day is very important for young goalies." – Jhonas Enroth

GLOVE

Any technical or physical skill that relates to your glove, including placement, positioning, reactions, and hand mechanics. This also includes sub-skills like the way you use your glove to trap pucks against your body, along the ice, or even behind your back! The save known as the windmill is considered by many goalie coaches to be one of the most natural and beautiful athletic movements in hockey. There are many ways to improve your glove-hand skills both on and off the ice, but never underestimate the value of playing baseball and other hand-and-ball sports!

BLOCKER

The ability to move and use your blocker to make saves. This includes blocker placement, blocker reactions, and all stick-hand mechanics like passing or going paddle-down. Goalies should use their blocker to steer pucks to the boards, to fill space in traffic and when moving around a screen, and even to bat a puck out of midair while falling backward. You can even trap pucks against your blocker by using your glove hand for support. But beware of the dreaded blocker lock! This happens when your blocker falls behind you or away from your hips, creating unnecessary holes, bad stick positioning, and sloppy movements. You can even trap pucks against your blocker by using your glove hand for support!

TECHNICAL

STICK

Any ability that relates to using your stick, including saving and passing. The stick is often called the goalie's most important piece of equipment because it's the most versatile, acting as both a defensive and offensive tool. A strong stick allows you to deflect pucks away from dangerous areas or direct them to the corners. Your stick also acts like a steering wheel; leading with it allows you to make crisp, more direct pushes while maintaining balance. Good stickwork includes strong passing skills that can give your team key advantages, such as keeping possession of the puck, getting assists with transition passes—and in rare occasions—even scoring an empty-net goal!

LEG PADS

All of the skills that relate to the leg pads, including saves like the two-pad stack and the kick save, as well as how you use your leg pads to fill space. As equipment continues to slightly shrink at the NHL level, it becomes even more important for a goalie to be comfortable and protected in their gear, but always working to find ways to make it work more seamlessly with their legs and body. How do you like to modify your gear and make it better for your unique body and movements? Tinkering and simply wearing the gear is half the fun of being a goalie!

TECHNICAL

"It's so hard to win as a goalie. If there are hiccups along the way, you have to bounce back and stay strong. You can't hang your head."
– Evgeni Nabokov

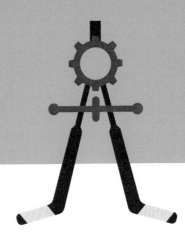

BUTTERFLY

The ability to flare out your leg pads and seal the lower portion of the net while keeping your head and body upright. The butterfly is the most common save in goaltending, but it's important to know that it's only a save selection—not a style. There are many variations of the basic butterfly save, including the compact or tight butterfly, the blocking butterfly, the half butterfly, and the wide butterfly. Even though you'll use the butterfly quite often due to its versatility and success rate, remember that it's just one of many ways to stop the puck!

POSITIONING

The ability to properly place your body between the puck and the net. Good positioning is the foundation of successful goaltending and is often explained as the combination of your depth, angle, and squareness. Positioning includes every part of your body—from your head to your hands to your toes—and it takes athleticism, agility, and good skating skills to get into the right spot at the right time. One way to find the correct position is to visualize a straight line starting from the center of the puck, going directly through your belly button, and then ending at the center of the net.

TECHNICAL

Save Selections

Sv

SAVE SELECTIONS

The collection of stances, techniques, and tactics that a goalie uses to make saves. As you develop, you'll build a set of skills and types of save selections that allow you to stop the puck in several ways. Therefore, it's important to know how to make the proper save in a given situation. While every goalie has their go-to save selections, you must always work on rounding out your skill-set by getting comfortable in executing as many types of saves as possible. The more balanced your save selections, the more dynamic and versatile a goalie you'll be!

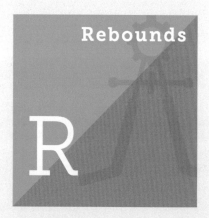

Rebounds

R

REBOUNDS

The ability to control a shot after making a save. Good rebounds happen when you deflect the puck away from everyone, often in the corners. Better rebounds happen when you put the puck in a spot where your teammates gain possession and can break out of the zone, maybe even turning up ice on a fast break. The best rebounds happen when you have full control of the puck after a save—from catching it, absorbing it with a gut trap, or reeling it in with your stick. Rebounds are a big part of the game and can be the difference between winning and losing, so practice directing pucks away from danger with your stick and steering them away with your hands. Good goalies stop rebounds, but great goalies eliminate them completely!

TECHNICAL

"If you think about the bad things, those are going to follow you around like a shadow. Sooner or later, a shadow is going to put you in the dark. Once I figured out that a support system and balance means a ton, it really made a difference in my game and my mental approach." – Brian Elliott

RECOVERIES

The ability to regain your feet or reset your stance. Whether it's an on-ice recovery for the purpose of making a back door push, or a full recovery after dropping into the butterfly too early, this element includes all types of recovery movements. Recoveries are a vital part of goaltending because goalies need to spend less time sliding and more time skating. Delayed recoveries can lead to a loss of body control and can force you to fall behind a play, so be sure to spend time working on all the ways you can regain your edges and quickly get back to your feet.

READING PLAYS

The ability to watch plays develop and anticipate how they'll unfold. Being able to read plays is critical to successful goaltending because it improves your positioning and leads to more efficient movements. This skill also includes the ability to recognize visual cues that can help you determine the best way to manage different situations, like odd-man rushes, shot types, and shooter tendencies. Goalies who excel at reading plays will often look calm, controlled, and effortless in their movements and reactions.

TECHNICAL

EDGES

EDGES

Any skill or technique related to using the inside or outside edges of your skates to move, react, and make saves. Whether you're on your feet or sliding on your knees, having quality edge control is a very important tool that stems from good footwork and skating skills. Many pro goalie coaches always preach "keep your feet" or "hold your edges" to help eliminate any chance of dropping too early. NHL goalies practice their edgework on a daily basis, which allows them to better alter their positioning and movements as quickly as possible.

CATCHING

CATCHING

The ability to catch a puck without giving up a rebound. Catching pucks cleanly is becoming a tougher skill to master, so you should place an emphasis on training your eye-hand coordination. Goalies must be able to catch a puck in a variety of ways, including in front of their face, across their chest and stomach, and even in front of their leg pads or just a few inches off the ice. In order to improve your catching skills, be sure to spend some time training with tennis balls and different types of sports vision goggles!

TECHNICAL

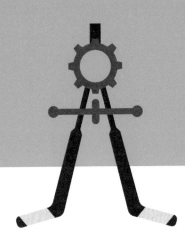

"Sometimes it's hard to put things behind you. But at the same time, the more you play, the more you learn how to do it and how to be ready for another challenge." – Pekka Rinne

WRIST ROLL

The ability to make blocker saves by rolling your wrist over and directing shots away from your body or from dangerous areas. The wrist roll is a sign of good body control, instincts, and technique. But not every blocker save should include a wrist roll—there are times when punching the puck away from traffic is a better decision. Whatever type of blocker save that you need to make, be sure to avoid blocker lock! Place your hands just in front of your hips and thighs and relax any tension in your arms. This helps activate your hands and improve your blocker reactions.

PASSING

The ability to pass the puck with your stick. There are two common passing techniques, including the traditional underhand grip and the more modern Turco grip, where the glove is turned over and placed on top of the stick shaft. Whether you're hitting a streaking teammate with a lead pass, making a soft chip around the boards, or using the high glass to ramp a puck up and out of the zone, passing is an extremely valuable skill to have in your toolbox. If you want to excel at passing, always keep your head up, find your targets quickly, and be aware of forecheckers!

TECHNICAL

SEALING ICE

The ability to create a complete seal to the ice with your pads and/or body. Sealing the ice is one of the most important duties for a goaltender because pucks should never go through or underneath you. Sealing the ice is extremely even more important when the puck is in tight to the crease area because it usually doesn't have the trajectory to elevate over your pad. If you seal the ice, you control the ice, and that gives you the best chance to make the save. Know how your pads work, snap your knees down hard to the ice, and create a strong seal to the ice whenever possible!

HALF BUTTERFLY

An essential, commonly used save selection that allows a goalie to extend one leg a greater distance than a full butterfly. By keeping one leg tucked under your body for support and stability, your other pad can extend further, faster. The half butterfly has a number of benefits over the course of a goalie's career, including less strain on the hips and groins. Note that you can execute this move in both forward and backward directions to come up with some big saves!

TECHNICAL

"You look at all those superhero movies, you don't start out being the best. They usually fall down and get back up. There's a reason for that. It mimics life a lot." – James Reimer

ANGLES

The ability to find the most efficient way to get the center of your body in between the puck and the net. Since the puck is always moving around the ice, playing the angles properly also requires an awareness of the play developing around them. This includes the ability to use lines on the ice (real or imaginary) and other visual cues to help you find the best possible angle for each situation. Goaltending is therefore a lot like geometry—it's the study of the lines and angles that arise from the constantly changing perspective between the shooter, puck, goalie, and net.

BLOCKING

The ability to make saves by transforming into a solid wall. This is done by sealing your arms to the side of your body and your gloves to the top of your pads. Your blocking wall can come in many shapes, sizes, and styles, so it's vital to know your coverage and block at the right time. No matter what your wall looks like, get as close to the puck as possible, stay upright, and try to keep your body relaxed. You can take your blocking skills to the next level by improving your decision-making and knowing when to block, when to react, and how to balance the use of both save selections!

TECHNICAL

Butterfly Slide

Bs

BUTTERFLY SLIDE

The ability to move laterally by pushing and sliding into a butterfly stance. This can be done by loading your weight onto an inside edge, rotating your hips and upper body, pushing off, and then controlling your slide as you move into a shot lane. It's crucial to have a good visual lead when butterfly-sliding, meaning that your head and eyes turn first, then your shoulders and hips in one fluid motion. It takes a lot of practice, repetition, and muscle memory in order to master the butterfly slide, and it's one of the main components to successful goaltending at the higher levels.

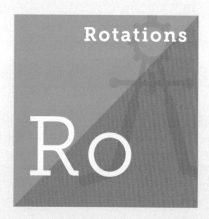

Rotations

Ro

ROTATIONS

The ability to rotate or swivel your hips in order to execute an on-ice recovery or a lateral adjustment. Having proper hip rotation will improve your overall positioning and movements while allowing you to square up to the puck more effectively. Rotating your hips often begins by turning your head and visually finding the spot where you want to go. Hip rotation should be done in a smooth and efficient manner, so turning your head and then your hips should happen in one fluid motion.

TECHNICAL

"A goalie must have one overriding quality - he must want to be a goalie."
– Emile Francis

PERIPHERAL VISION

The ability to see pucks and players out of the corners of your eyes. Being able to locate or follow what's happening at the edge of your field of vision can improve your anticipation, reads, and body control. Peripheral vision is an important skill to develop when scanning the ice for threats because you're no longer relying solely on your direct line of sight to gather valuable information. It's also important when focusing on a puck because you can still notice things that exist beyond the center of your gaze, like a player coming off the bench or a sneaky backdoor threat!

LATERAL ADJUSTMENT

Any movement that results in a lateral angle change. Lateral adjustments include pre- and post-save movements, made both on your feet and on your knees. For example, you can do a lateral adjustment while standing through the use of a T-push, C-cut, shuffle, or hop-step. On your knees, you can do it with a butterfly slide or backside push. Lateral adjustments include pre- and post-save movements, made both on your feet and on your knees. Lateral adjustments also include the sub-skill known as a lateral release, which is done in order to eliminate any over-sliding. By holding their edges a little longer, a goalie is able to drive their knees down under control and without losing squareness to the puck.

TECHNICAL

ACTIVE HANDS

The ability to activate and move your hands in order to improve your net coverage. This includes doing whatever you can with your glove, blocker, or stick to take away a shooter's time and space. Having active hands allows goalies to cut off cross-crease passes, take away open lanes, eliminate aerial angles, and gain proximity on the puck by pushing their gloves forward. With the rising skill of today's shooters, using active hands is more important than ever before. You must always work hard to keep your hands loose, relaxed, placed slightly in front of your body, and in a set and ready position.

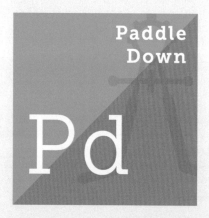

PADDLE DOWN

The ability to place the paddle of your stick along the ice in order to seal the 5-hole and make saves. The paddle-down is most commonly used on jams, walkouts, wraparounds, and scramble plays close to the net. This technique can also be used to reach back and stop a puck from crossing the goal line, or on a breakaway when the shooter tries to elevate or flip a puck close to the crease. Once your paddle is sealed to the ice, try extending your entire stick forward in order to take away time and space from the shooter so that a puck can't sneak or slide by you!

TECHNICAL

"Sometimes you do everything right and the puck still goes in."
– Tony Esposito

POKE CHECK

The ability to fully or partially extend your stick in order to poke the puck off a shooter's stick. There are many ways to poke away a loose puck that's lying in or close to the crease, so goalies must be able to master the ability to read plays and have proper timing. Goalies must know when to poke and when to "stay home" and not get caught overreaching or overextending their arm and creating larger holes. Like many other technical elements, the key to success with the poke check is to do it with quickness and unpredictability!

KICK SAVES

The ability to make a save by kicking the puck away from danger. These are also called toe saves, but both terms include the ability to get the boot break of your pad or the toe of your skate on a puck and then kick it away. One trademark of the traditional kick save is turning the toe of your skate blade up and digging into the ice with your heel as you make the save. Kick saves are often considered old school by today's standards because they were a very popular save selection in the 1970s all the way until the introduction of the butterfly in the early 1990s.

TECHNICAL

VH Stance

Vh

VH STANCE

A post integration technique where one leg is sealed vertically against the post while the other is placed horizontally along the ice; hence, the "VH." You could use the VH stance should be used only when the puck is at a dead angle and close to the crease. It's important for young goalies to understand the when, where, and why for this save selection because it's easy to overuse the VH as a result of reading the play incorrectly.

Depth

Dp

DEPTH

Your body's proximity to the puck in relation to the goal line. Optimal depth depends primarily on the size of your body, the puck's location, and the situation. Extreme depth occurs when your body is covering more area than necessary, thus having longer distances to travel when recovering back to either post. A lack of depth occurs when you fail to challenge properly and can't cover enough space with your body. Whether you like to be more aggressive or conservative with your depth, both can be effective, so take the time to find out what works best for you!

TECHNICAL

"The day you think you can't get any better is the day you'll see your competition ahead of you." – Henrik Lundqvist

CHALLENGE

The ability to read a shooter and then change your depth by moving closer to the puck or taking away their time and space. Challenging the shooter increases your net coverage and can help eliminate holes by closing gaps. It's also referred to as "gaining depth" with the body or "projecting" the hands forward or over the puck. Gap control is another term that's often used when discussing how to manage breakaways, and knowing when and how to challenge is an essential part of establishing your initial positioning and then controlling the gap as the puck carrier approaches.

BACKSIDE PUSH

The ability to rotate your head, hands, and hips and then push off with your back skate in order to laterally adjust your positioning. This technique can be done a few ways. A good backside push can lead to a full recovery back to your feet, end with your body hugging the post, or by finishing out your push and moving again from there. Looking where you want to go, having proper knee elevation, squaring up your shoulders, leading with your hands, and having good balance are some of the keys to executing an effective backside push.

TECHNICAL

WEIGHT TRANSFER

The ability to change directions by transferring your weight from side to side in order to move, react, or alter your positioning. Whether you're shifting your upper body or butterfly-sliding, you must use your inside edges to change or reverse your current path. You can properly execute a weight transfer by loading your weight onto one leg, pushing off your skate blade, and then channeling your weight to the other side of your body. Like athletes in other sports, a goalie's feet and core muscles are the power cell of their body and the control center of weight transfers.

SCANNING

The ability to shift your gaze and quickly survey the ice in order to see what's happening away from the puck. Goalies do this so that they can discover where other players are, where potential threats could come from, and what options dangerous shooters may have. Scanning can be done by looking over your shoulder, across your body, or anywhere else in the defensive zone. It's a great skill to add to your game and can vastly improve your ability to anticipate, so get in the habit of taking a quick look to see what's happening away from the puck!

THE PERIODIC TABLE – of – GOALTENDING ELEMENTS

TECHNICAL

"The one thing I've learned about being a pro is the importance of making sure you show up every day to compete." – Richard Bachman

HOP-STEP

An advanced lateral movement that deepens the goalie's toolbox beyond the three main skating movements of the shuffle, T-push, and C-cut. The hop-step occurs when a goalie lifts one skate off the ice and hops laterally with their drive foot in order to quickly adjust their positioning. This movement takes time to master, but when done properly, reduces friction and drag while also keeping you upright on your skates and fully square to the puck. The hop-step was popularized by Jack Campbell and many other American-born goalies.

DEFLECTIONS

The ability to effectively read and react to pucks that are tipped, redirected, or deflected. Success in this area requires proper visual attachment, tracking, and reading of aerial angles. Making saves on deflections also means being able to anticipate a shot's changed trajectory and reading the alteration speed of a puck that hits a stick blade, skate, or body part after it's already been released. Managing deflections also takes great body control and instincts, as these shots often result in the need for you to quickly change or re-react to a different spot.

TECHNICAL

Gut Trap

Gt

GUT TRAP

The ability to trap pucks against your stomach area without allowing a rebound. This seems like a simple skill to have in your toolbox, but at the higher levels, absorbing or cradling shots against the body is an art form that can prevent scoring chances. Being able to corral heavy, tricky shots off your shoulders, arms, and chest area takes strong body awareness and body angling. For example, knowing exactly how to make the small movements like collapsing your arms, breaking or flexing your hips, or even sensing how to cushion (soften) your body is a key part of executing a proper gut trap.

Stick on Puck

Sp

STICK ON PUCK

The ability to get your stick blade on the puck in order to deflect it away from danger. This includes the ability to clear a puck up off the glass, deflect it out of play, or quickly swat it away when it falls off your body. Getting stick-on-puck is crucial for shots along the ice because bad rebounds are more likely to come off your leg pads and land in high-percentage scoring areas in front of the net. One way to improve your stick-on-puck is by tracking the puck into your body and keeping your hands relaxed as you "mirror" the puck with your stick blade, then following through as it leads into your next movement or recovery.

TECHNICAL

"My focus was always first and foremost to stop the puck. I never let the other players on the other team get to me." – Andy Moog

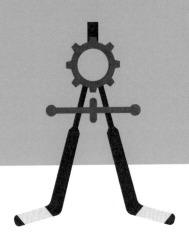

LONGBODY

The ability to extend your lead skate toward the puck while laying your body on the ice. The longbody technique seals the ice with your pad and body, building coverage upward with the use of active hands. This effective desperation save selection is usually seen on rebounds, backdoor chances, and breakaways, but can also be used whenever a more efficient save selection will not cover enough net. Staying compact and in control is always the focus of goaltending, but in desperate situations, don't be afraid to let loose and use the longbody to stop the puck!

REVERSE VH

RVH for short, the Reverse VH is a popular post integration technique used for sealing the post. As the opposite of the traditional VH position, one pad is placed along the ice (horizontal) while your back leg is anchored into the ice with your skate's inside edge (vertical) so that your body can push into the post, thus creating a stronger seal. There are different ways to seal the post in the RVH, including using your toe bridge, your skate on the post, and the "shin-on-post" technique. No matter which variation you prefer, it's crucial to know how to execute all three of them and when to use each one!

TECHNICAL

SQUARENESS

The ability to properly align all parts of your body to the center of the puck. Squareness takes strong positioning (angle plus depth) and good body control in order to properly set your head, shoulders, knees, and toes. Squaring up to the puck is an important skill because it makes your body as big as possible to the puck and removes your need to overreach or overreact. One way to optimize your squareness is by making sure that your head is slightly over your body when a shot is taken so that you don't get caught falling off the puck or pulling away from the shot line at the last second.

TRANSITIONS

The ability to move efficiently and with control from one stance to the next. Good transitions are a result of good timing and decision-making; you need to know exactly what type of transition to make and what stance to move into, and then you need to do it at the right time. Combined with proper technique, transitions are an effective way to execute your game plan and manage different situations within a game. Transitions constantly take place in a game, like when you move in and out of the butterfly, recover back to your skates, or go from the VH to the Reverse VH stance.

TECHNICAL

"Nobody understands the position who hasn't played it. Hockey is a team game, but for a goalie, it's more like an individual sport." – John Garrett

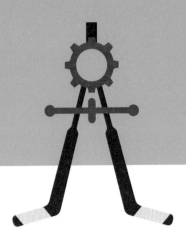

SHOULDER SHRUGS

The ability to react, lift, flex, or shrug your shoulders in order to make a save. When a goalie drops into the butterfly a moment too soon on an elevated shot, a shoulder shrug can help eliminate some space in the upper portion of the net. It can also help keep their body upright instead of falling forward with "dead" or inactive arms. The shoulder shrug is vital on dead-angle shots, as your shoulders, chest, and head need to be in a forward position so that the puck deflects down toward the ice or into your body—and not back and up like a ramp into the net.

KNEE WALKS

The ability to keep sealing the ice by pushing one knee beyond your hip and then pulling the trailing knee back underneath you. This is often executed rapidly and in succession, allowing you to stay upright and mobile without lifting a knee or creating a hole. Knee walks are also called "shimmies" or "knee shuffles" because the goalie is shuffling or quickly moving laterally in order to better manage their squareness to the puck. Knee walks take good core strength and body awareness, as well as strong thighs and hamstrings.

TECHNICAL

Reading
Releases

Rr

READING RELEASES

The ability to process information about a shooter's release. This includes being able to assess information on the movement and angle of the stick blade, the type of release, the trajectory of the puck as it leaves the stick blade, and any other visual cues that might help you anticipate and react to a shot. Reading releases is an advanced skill because it takes experience to know how to process all types of releases that you'll see. Shots are more deceptive than ever before, so this skill can give you an edge on opponents as you get older.

Heel Lift

Hl

HEEL LIFT

Also known as a scorpion save, this extremely rare save selection takes place when a goalie is on their stomach, but in a desperate effort to make a save, they lift the heel of their skate(s) off the ice in order to get a piece of a rising shot. On February 9th, 2012 against the San Jose Sharks, Miikka Kiprusoff made a legendary heel-lift save in his 300th career win. The heel-lift save is a sign of elite awareness, agility, battle, and second-effort play. It's considered a desperation save, but can be calculated and done with a purpose. On February 9th, 2012 against the San Jose Sharks, Miikka Kiprusoff made a legendary heel-lift save in his 300th career win.

TACTICAL

"

"You're going to have opportunities to be whatever you want and do whatever you want. It doesn't matter what background you have, who does or doesn't like you, or what part of the country you're from. It's all up to you. Go write your own story."

– SCOTT DARLING

TACTICAL

"I really think it is so important to self-visualize. In the back of your mind you've been there a little bit, and you feel a little more prepared for those situations." – Chris Mason

AERIAL ANGLES

The ability to read, process, and manage rising shots. This tactic not only refers to your ability to track a puck as it elevates off the ice, but also where your body should be positioned and where your hands should be placed as a result. You can discuss and study aerial angles with your goalie coach by going over video that was shot from the puck's perspective along the ice. As a rule of thumb, you can eliminate an aerial angle by moving your gloves and stick (or other parts of your body) toward the puck to cut off the puck's angle to the net. This is often referred to as "projecting" or "closing in" on a puck.

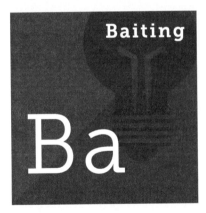

BAITING

The ability to expose a specific or small space and purposely leave it unguarded in order to mislead, or "bait," a shooter to aim for that exact spot. This advanced tactic can be used in a variety of ways, but it's usually seen on breakaways and in shootouts. Henrik Lundqvist, for example, is known for baiting shooters to his blocker side by making a quick-twitch reaction on purpose, or by over-positioning himself slightly to his glove side. Similarly, Patrick Roy was known for baiting shooters to aim for his 5-hole.

TACTICAL

TRAFFIC PLAY

The ability to play your game through traffic and screens. Every goalie does this differently, but a rule of thumb is to either look over a screen by staying more upright, or get extra low and look through or around them. In both cases, the goal is to work as hard as you can to keep your eyes on the puck. Other skills in this realm include reading a shot release through layers of bodies, center-shifting into a partially screened shot lane while losing sight of the puck for a split second, and anticipating redirections as bodies move across your field of vision.

TWO-PAD STACK

The ability to cover a good portion of the net by laying on your side and stacking your leg pads on top of each other. The two-pad stack is a lost art and rare sight in today's game, but is still one of the most appreciated movements in goaltending. When done properly, it can surprise a shooter and suddenly take away space in both the upper and lower parts of the net, despite the goalie appearing to be down and out on a play. You can also increase your coverage by stacking your free arm on top of your top pad. You may not find yourself using the two-pad stack very often, but every goalie should keep this save selection in their toolbox because there will be a time when it works so well that fans and teammates erupt with excitement!

TACTICAL

"I don't fear stopping a 100 MPH slap shot, I fear not stopping it."
– Roberto Luongo

OVERLAP

An advanced post coverage tactic that's executed by staying upright and overlapping your skate with the goal post. By placing your skate just outside of the post by a few (or many) inches, you increase your options and will have a more relaxed, patient stance when reading dead-angle plays. Because you're no longer anchored to the post, you have the freedom to butterfly, transition into the VH or Reverse VH, or execute a backside push. Overlapping also allows for full vertical coverage with a taller torso, square shoulders, and less strain on your hips and knees.

BOX CONTROL

The ability to choose the most efficient stance and body positioning needed to have perfect net coverage from the puck's point of view. Box control is playing in relation to the imaginary net directly in front of you—not how much net is open behind you. You can develop this tactic in many ways, but a popular one is by using a video camera along the ice with ropes tied to either post to help you see and understand the true space available from the puck's perspective. So, box control isn't only a tactic for mastering your angles and depth, but a method of teaching as well.

TACTICAL

NUDGES

A subtle movement in the direction of the puck, usually occurring after you've already set your feet. When you recognize that you have time and space to nudge slightly in the direction of the shot's path, it can greatly benefit your net coverage and overall positioning. A nudge can also occur laterally or while your feet are still moving, so it can also be referred to as a forward release. Either way, it's important to remember that nudges are very small adjustments—a little bit of movement goes a long way!

BUMPS

The ability to use your skate blade, toe bridge, boot break, or shin of your pad to push off the post and "bump" to the other side. This advanced lateral adjustment is a tactical move that's often used while in the Reverse VH or full butterfly. It allows a goalie to keep the ice sealed with their knees and leg pads while still moving from post to post and filling space to the far side. Bumps improve your ability to manage plays below the goal line and will enhance your positioning when the puck is behind the net, but they require core strength and proper weight transfers in order to be effective.

THE PERIODIC TABLE – *of* – GOALTENDING ELEMENTS

TACTICAL

"Only a goalie can appreciate what a goalie goes through."
– Jacques Plante

Pop-Up Recovery

Pu

POP-UP RECOVERY

The ability to recover from the butterfly and back up to both of your feet in one fluid motion. This is done by pulling your knees off the ice at the same time and popping up into your ready stance. This advanced technique takes a lot of core strength and agility to execute properly, but can be an effective recovery tactic and a great addition to a goalie's toolbox. The main advantage of the pop-up recovery is that it can allow for a quicker reset than a traditional full recovery, which is done by recovering on one foot and then the other.

Head Trajectory

Ht

HEAD TRAJECTORY

The ability to optimize your puck-tracking skills by positioning and moving your head in a more functional manner. "Head trajectory" is currently trademarked by goalie coach Lyle Mast, who has developed an effective training method and tactics system behind the skill. On a basic level, though, head trajectory can refer to anything related to the movement of your head in order to better focus on the puck. Head trajectory is often accompanied by the phrase "tracking down," which means tilting your head forward so that the center of your gaze is directly on top of the middle of the puck.

TACTICAL

MICRO ADJUSTMENTS

The ability to make slight adjustments with different parts of your body in order to improve positioning, coverage, or squareness. Goalies who make good micro-adjustments are advanced thinkers and athletes; they read the play extremely well, demonstrate great spatial recognition skills, and have strong attention to detail. Micro-adjustments are harder to master than micro-movements due to their combination of cognitive abilities; not only are you making a small movement, but you're also executing an actual adjustment of your angle, depth, or body positioning.

SCRAMBLING

The ability to move your body and execute your game plan with urgency and at a high speed in order to make saves. Scrambling is different from desperation because effective scrambling means that you maintain good control of your body and still move with a purpose. It's often considered "controlled athleticism" in the sense that a goalie can move in a hurry to stop the puck in the midst of a broken, chaotic, or uncontrolled situation. Goalie coaches will often dedicate time to run scrambling drills in order to help their goalies find a higher level of comfort in these situations.

TACTICAL

"I play a position where you make mistakes. The only people that don't make them at a hockey game are the people watching." – Patrick Roy

Anticipation

Ai

ANTICIPATION

The ability to predict a shot or play before it actually occurs. As goalies get better at reading plays and seeing how they develop, they can spend less time guessing and more time getting set before a shot is taken. A few ways to improve your anticipation are by reading the shooter's stick blade position (open or closed) and the puck's location on the blade (toe or heel). You can also improve this skill by practicing in small-area games because they challenge you to respect the puck carrier, make patient reads, and constantly scan the ice for potential scoring threats.

Contorting

Cn

CONTORTING

The ability to purposefully place your body in a vulnerable, extreme, or strained position in order to make a save. This type of movement is made by relying mostly on natural flexibility, agility, and grit. Contorting saves can be unconventional and even downright painful. One of the best examples of contorting is when a goalie drops into the full-blown splits in order to make a save on a breakaway. Legends like Dominik Hasek, Tim Thomas, and Jonathan Quick are widely considered to be three of the best contortionists in the history of the NHL.

TACTICAL

Sr
Spatial Recognition

SPATIAL RECOGNITION

The ability to use an enhanced awareness of your surroundings and place in space to improve your performance. Spatial recognition is an advanced mental and physical skill that develops over time and as you become more in tune with your body. It's an enhancement of all five senses that allows you to better position your body, read the play, and anticipate shots. The more you can sense and feel your exact position on the ice, how much net you're covering, or where you are in relation to the puck, the better you'll be at making saves and taking away a shooter's time and space!

Di
Displacement

DISPLACEMENT

An effective tactic for improving your net coverage through a screen or traffic. Displacement is accomplished by filling open space around a screen or body by placing your glove or blocker to the opposite side of your body. For example, if you lean to your blocker side to see around a screen, you "displace" the glove by positioning it away from your body and on the other side of the screen. On the other hand, if you lean to your glove side, you displace the blocker by extending it away from your body so that it fills space on the other side of the screen.

TACTICAL

"Some people get paralyzed by the pressure, but elite goalies get motivated by it." – Mitch Korn

PATTERN RECOGNITION

Pr
Pattern Recognition

The ability to recognize the many patterns within the game of hockey. Over time and through sheer repetition, elite goalies are able to read and process these regularities, even ones with subtle variations. They're able to spot deceptive shot releases, read the hand and blade curve of a player's stick, anticipate certain passes on penalty kills or odd-man rushes, and predict what move a player will likely use in a shootout. Pattern recognition is developed over time and through pure desire, so the more you play, the better you'll become at reading the game and seeing the patterns.

PUCK MANAGEMENT

Pm
Puck Management

The ability to manage pucks around the crease area, specifically in uncontrolled situations. Puck management is an intangible skill, meaning that it is not directly related to making saves. Still, it does a number of things to alleviate pressure around the crease, like covering loose pucks, directing pucks away from opponents and to teammates or the corners, playing the puck, or settling a fluttering puck when it's flipping or moving in unpredictable ways. Good puck management also means making an effort to get quick whistles from the referee when your team needs a line change, which helps take the pressure off your teammates and lets everyone catch their breath.

TACTICAL

Barrel Roll

Br

BARREL ROLL

Often called a "Hasek Roll" due to originator Dominik Hasek, this move is rarely seen in today's game. It takes place when a goalie executes a two-pad stack and then lifts their legs and hands off the ice in order to make a 180-degree vertical rotation of their pads and gloves. This keeps the ice sealed with the body, but eliminates space on the opposite side of the net. The pads make an aerial sweep like a giant windshield wiper, taking away the upper part of the net, while the hands and arms can either stay locked to the body or projected toward the puck.

Post Integration

Pi

POST INTEGRATION

The ability to move your body into position against the posts. There are many ways to integrate into or against the posts in order to cover space, including sliding or dropping from a standstill position. Whether you decide to use the VH, the Reverse VH, the overlap, or another variation of these common stances, you must learn how to move into post coverage quickly and comfortably. This takes good flexibility, and body awareness with the positioning of your skate blade, hips, arms, and shoulder.

TACTICAL

"To live in the moment, I think that comes from just learning about yourself, and learning to know that there's only so much you can do as a goalie. I never met a person that could change the past, and at the end of the day, that's hockey." – Niklas Backstrom

GAME PLAN

The ability to add more structure to your game by establishing a plan for your playing style and tactics. This is usually done by writing down and diagramming what stances or techniques you want to use in different situations. Specifically, most goalies will draw lines on a blank rink diagram and explain where they would be positioned when the puck is in different zones on the ice. Game-planning is also referred to as game-mapping because you visibly map out your positioning, techniques, and stances for a more consistent approach to how you execute your game.

GAP CONTROL

The ability to manage the amount of space between the puck, your body, and the goal line. Gap control is often mentioned when practicing breakaways, odd-man rushes, or most plays where a skater carries the puck into the offensive zone. It's comprised of many elements in the Technical category, including challenging, depth, timing, and your ability to read plays. One of the most common ways to work on your gap control is by trying to match the speed of the shooter when retreating or backing up on a breakaway.

TACTICAL

HINGING

The ability to swivel and rotate your body forward or backward while covering the post in the Reverse VH position. Hinging forward closes off aerial angles and improves net coverage while staying sealed to the post. Hinging backward allows a goalie to bump across the goal line in a more efficient manner. Hinging backward is often called "flattening out" because the goalie becomes flatter along the goal line. Hinging in both directions takes great edges, body control, and agility. The more you lean into the post with your shoulder, arm, and foot, the easier it can be to hinge both ways!

ADAPTIVE SKATING

The ability to use your edges and skating skills in order to regain proper positioning after an initial play has left you off-balance. When the game forces you into a bad or tricky spot, adaptive skating allows you to quickly recover and regain control of your body and angles. This is often accomplished by using small forward or backward C-cuts and other similar skating movements, especially into or off of the posts. You will also see goalies use adaptive skating in tight spaces or during scramble situations around the crease area.

TACTICAL

"You don't have to be crazy to play goal, but it helps."
– Bernie Parent

QUIET EYE

The ability to focus your gaze on the puck for the moments before, during, and directly after a shot is released. This theory, which was originated by scientist Joan Vickers and her work at the University of Calgary, was able to prove that the quiet eye is a teachable skill. Through her research, she discovered a direct correlation between save percentages and the intensity of a goalie's eye contact with the puck before it's shot. The longer the attention span on that small area of ice (down to a few hundred milliseconds), the better the goalie reaction speeds.

ANGLE MANAGEMENT

The ability to analyze and manage your angles with pure efficiency. This is done by using all of your mental, technical, and physical skills to stay perfectly on angle without over-challenging or losing squareness to the puck. Proper angle management includes the ability to rapidly change your positioning by having good edges and skills like micro-adjustments. By analyzing what angles could be created on different shot releases and odd-man rushes, you can better anticipate the play, letting you focus more on managing angles and less on technical execution.

TACTICAL

ENERGY MANAGEMENT

The ability to reduce the strain and stress on your body over the course of a game, season, or lengthy career. Managing energy is vital for workhorse goalies who play heavy minutes, and it's an aspect of the game that's becoming more important. Managing energy not only includes how economically you move on the ice (see Economical and Efficiency), but also how you manage off-ice aspects of development like sleep, nutrition, hydration, stretching, strength training, your social life, and the amount of stress your mind and body experiences on a daily basis.

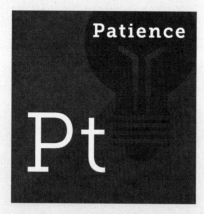

PATIENCE

The ability to maintain your positioning and body movements until the right moment. Patience is a virtue, meaning that it includes the Mental category as well as the Physical. Patience is required at the higher levels in order to stay on angle and square to the shot. It's also known as the ability to let the shooter make the first move on a breakaway. Patient goalies let the game and pucks come to them—they don't over-anticipate plays by reacting or dropping early. Holding your edges, out-waiting the shooter, and staying on your feet for shots are just a few examples of patience!

TACTICAL

"I always make sure to tell my goalies that many people could live their whole life without being aware of their breathing, but the best athletes I've coached and read about, they manage their breathing very well."
– Erik Granqvist

BREATHING

The ability to use advanced breathing techniques in order to improve performance. Not only can good breathing habits help regulate your nervous system, but training in this tactic can help you stay relaxed and calm in pressure-filled situations. Proper breathing can also help you clear your mind and reset, stabilize your muscular system, and even help you stay focused and in control when you're tired or suffering from fatigue. There are also many ways to improve your athletic breathing skills, including off-ice functional movement disciplines like yoga and Pilates!

KINESTHETIC SENSE

The exceptional ability of knowing exactly which part of your body to move and how to move it in any given situation. This heightened sense of awareness is external, meaning that it relates to your place in time and space. At the highest levels, goalies rarely have time to make conscious decisions and reactions, so they have to rely on natural body awareness and proprioception (inner senses) to determine precisely what direction and speed to move certain body parts. Kinesthetic sense is a deep, intuitive skill that comes only with years of experience and takes a lifetime to master.

Design Your Gear!

Thanks to Mash over at PadsTracker, you can design your dream gear and share it with the rest of the goalie world! Color in these blank templates and then tag **@PadsTracker** and **@TheGoalieGuild** on Instagram or Twitter with a photo of your creation!

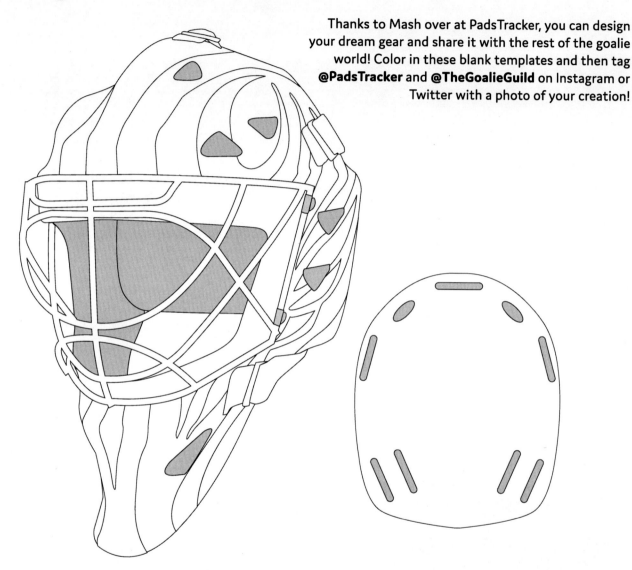

COURTESY OF MATHEW ABRAHAM AT THEGOALIEARCHIVE.COM

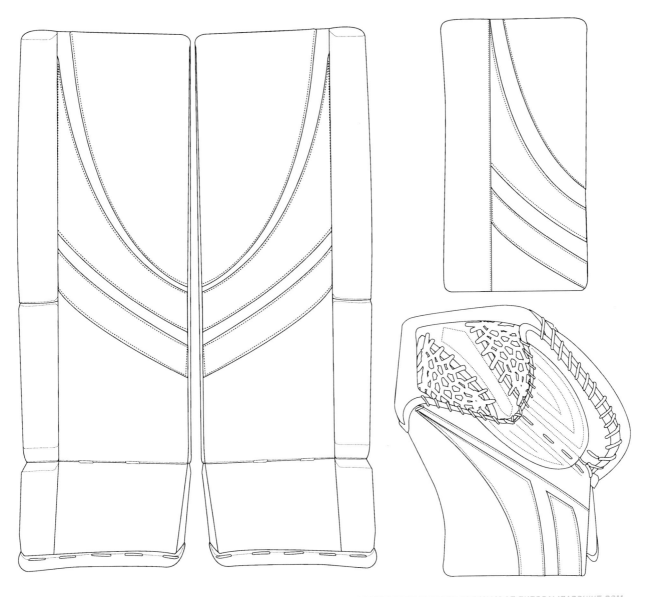

COURTESY OF MATHEW ABRAHAM AT THEGOALIEARCHIVE.COM

THE PERIODIC TABLE – of – GOALTENDING ELEMENTS

Build Your Own Table

Take a crack at designing your very own goaltending periodic table by placing elements wherever you'd like. You can even add new elements, or change the table's appearance and layout!

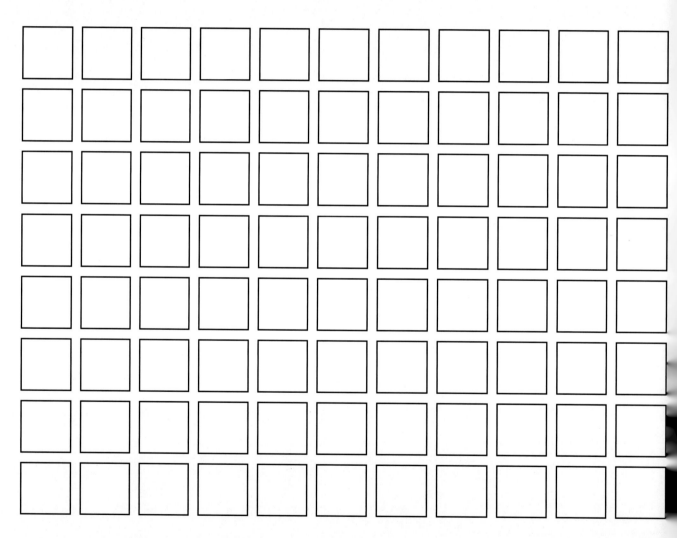

THE PERIODIC TABLE – of – GOALTENDING ELEMENTS

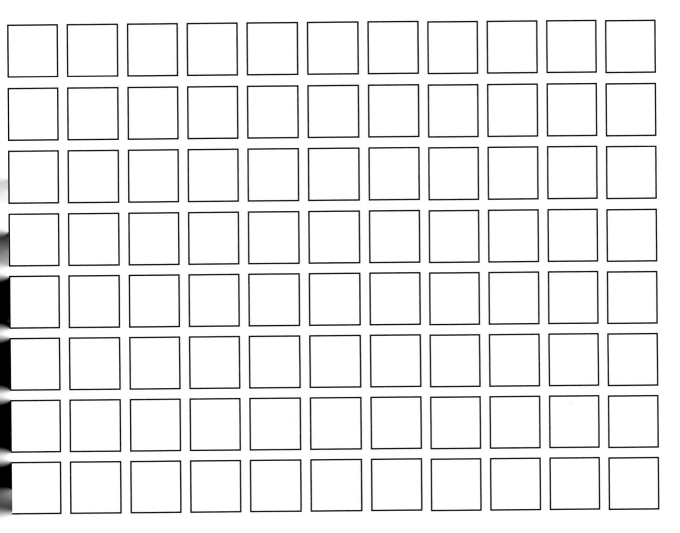

THE PERIODIC TABLE – *of* – GOALTENDING ELEMENTS

Building Your Foundation

Visualize your unique goaltending identity by writing in the different elements that make up your foundation. This can be any arrangement of mental, technical, or physical skills that makes you unique. **Be creative!**

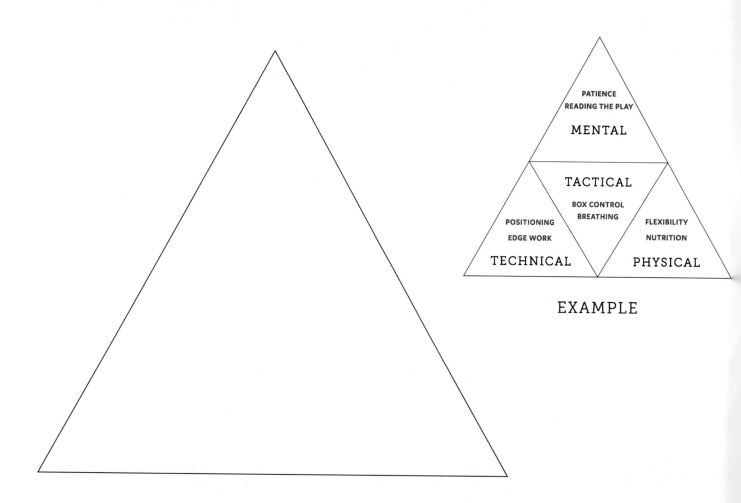

MENTAL

PATIENCE
READING THE PLAY

TACTICAL

BOX CONTROL
BREATHING

POSITIONING
EDGE WORK

TECHNICAL

FLEXIBILITY
NUTRITION

PHYSICAL

EXAMPLE

THE PERIODIC TABLE – *of* – GOALTENDING ELEMENTS

Have a Purpose

Work Ethic is not only a necessary part of every goalie's foundation, it's a key to success in all areas of life. Its influence on an athlete's overall talent is never underestimated by any coach or scout, and no matter who you are, it will become one of the most important skills in your toolbox.

Developing a strong Work Ethic is anything but easy. It demands every ounce of your energy at times, it requires sacrifices of time and other pleasures, and it won't produce immediate results.

It will, however, bear many fruits. It will lay the groundwork for all of your physical and mental abilities. It will also give you the chance to thrive on your desires and motivations, pushing you forward and inching you closer to your goals. It will extend your boundaries, raise your talent ceiling, and elevate those around you.

A goalie's **Work Ethic** is being tested every day, especially when no one is watching. Even though it may be tough at times and cause setbacks, you must choose to learn from every moment. Ultimately, those that stay the course and trust the process will ultimately succeed.

Since 1999, Bandits Goalie School has been producing quality goaltenders in the heart of Michigan. Over the years, the coaching staff has instilled a phrase and ideology in every student, one that positively influences their daily mindset and brings their lives more meaning.

The term is Have A Purpose.

Its aim? To create a higher sense of meaning in everything they do, both on and off the ice.

It's a verbal vehicle that drives your desire to be successful. It is echoed in all that you do and it propels you towards your core principles, goals, motivations, and more importantly, closer to YOU! It also reminds you that your work ethic will influence the way you apply yourself in all aspects of life's daily tasks: athletics, school, family, and your personal life.

Work Ethic requires certain personality traits that define your unique identity, not only as a goalie, but what you stand for. These traits transcend sports, because they make up who you are as a teammate, classmate, coworker, and individual in society. They define your purpose.

Character: Goalies with a strong work ethic often possess strong character. Traits such as being internally driven, self-disciplined, and task-oriented prove they have a purpose. These athletes are honest and dependable, and they apply these distinctive leadership traits on a daily basis, separating themselves from the competition.

Accountability: Goalies with a strong work ethic hold themselves responsible for their actions in every situation, proving there is a purpose to their choices. They exhibit Mindfulness and never make excuses when things don't go as planned. They acknowledge their mistakes and use them as learning experiences. They also expect others around them to meet the same level of standards in order to keep them accountable and reliable.

Dedication: Goalies with a strong work ethic are dedicated to their craft and will go to great lengths to make certain that they perform when called upon. Being dedicated often means putting in extra hours beyond what is expected of you, proving there is a purpose to your actions. It will not always be recognized or praised, but your dedication will build an internal force that won't break when things break down around you.

As you can see, your work ethic plays a pivotal role in your success each and every day. By remembering to Have A Purpose and bring passion to all that you do, it will only make you stronger. By staying true to yourself and your purpose, you will develop the positive attitude needed to achieve greatness on a daily basis. Those who choose to embrace a strong work ethic at an early age will dominate, lead, and succeed!

- Coach Joe Messina

Reflection Questions

1. How would you define your purpose?

_____

_____

_____

_____

2. How do you plan on living out your purpose?

_____

_____

_____

_____

3. What can you do to improve your work ethic?

_____

_____

_____

_____

4. In what areas of the game can you work harder?

_____

_____

_____

_____

5. Is there someone in your life that has an admirable work ethic? Why?

_____

_____

_____

_____

About the Author

Since 2007, Justin Goldman has been contributing to the goaltending community. After establishing The Goalie Guild (a 501-c3 nonprofit foundation) in 2009, he spent four years (2011-14) writing weekly goalie articles for the NHL.com website. In 2013, he joined USA Hockey as a goalie consultant, mentor, and director for various national and local development programs. During his three-year tenure with USA Hockey, Justin traveled around the world to study the position and went on to publish his first three books, **The Power Within** (2014), **Between Two Worlds** (2015), and **Embracing The Grind** (2016). Beyond his duties with The Goalie Guild, Goldman also acts as the director of operations for NetWork Goaltending and a consultant for numerous pro, junior, and college hockey teams.

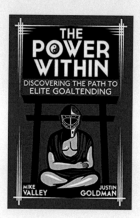  

About the Designer

Kathy Polo is a freelance graphic artist and storyteller. Fueled by her passion for hockey and the communities surrounding the game, Kathy Polo has dedicated her career to inspire, educate and communicate via design. She has worked with clients big and small to create animated GIF's, explainer videos, illustrations, infographics and more. Her work has been featured on TSN, Sportsnet, Fast Company, Yahoo! Sports and other online platforms. You can find more of her work, as well as updates about upcoming projects, on her website: **katyapolo.com**.

83638224R00058

Made in the USA
San Bernardino, CA
28 July 2018